William Pitt, man Honest

A Letter to the Right Honourable William Pitt

on his apostacy from the cause of parliamentary reform - to which is

subjoined an appendix containing important documents on that subject.

Second Edition

William Pitt, man Honest

A Letter to the Right Honourable William Pitt
on his apostacy from the cause of parliamentary reform - to which is subjoined an appendix containing important documents on that subject. Second Edition

ISBN/EAN: 9783337195649

Printed in Europe, USA, Canada, Australia, Japan

Cover: Foto ©Andreas Hilbeck / pixelio.de

More available books at **www.hansebooks.com**

A LETTER

TO THE RIGHT HONOURABLE

WILLIAM PITT,

ON

HIS APOSTACY

FROM THE CAUSE OF

PARLIAMENTARY REFORM.

TO WHICH IS SUBJOINED

AN APPENDIX,

CONTAINING

IMPORTANT DOCUMENTS

ON THAT SUBJECT.

Audax venali comitatur CURIO linguâ
Vox quondam Populi libertatemque tueri
Ausus!——

THE SECOND EDITION.

LONDON:

PRINTED FOR H. D. SYMONDS,

PATERNOSTER-ROW.

1793.

ADVERTISEMENT.

PUBLICATIONS *on fugitive topics, though from their nature sometimes lefs dubioufly ufeful to mankind than more permanent works, are fo little a fource of reputation, that their Authors have commonly thought it prudent to withold their names. If an Author be obfcure, fuch publications will not exalt him—if he be eminent, they may be fuppofed to derogate from the gravity of more ferious occupations, or from the dignity of a more folid fame.*

Thefe common reafons may be fufficient for anonymous publication, efpecially in a cafe like the prefent, which confifts either of argument, which a name can neither ftrengthen nor impair ; or of facts, which are fo acknowledged as to need no teftimony for their fupport.

The Author may be fuppofed by fome to owe an apology for the feverity of the language which he has fometimes ufed.—The only language, however, which he could have ufed, on fuch an occafion, was that of indignant honefty. He could neither palliate truth, nor compromife virtue ; nor does he profefs to emulate thofe Courtly Writers, the gentlenefs of whofe cenfures almoft mitigates guilt into innocence.

A LETTER

TO THE

RIGHT HONOURABLE

WILLIAM PITT,

&c. &c.

Audax venali Comitatur Curio linguâ
Vox quondam Populi libertatemque tueri
Aufus——
    Lucan Pharsalia, *Lib. i. l.* 269—71.

SIR,

HISTORY records too many examples of political apoftacy to make any cafe of that fort new or fingular. Yet with all your knowledge in that branch of hiftory, to which congenial fentiments muft have naturally pointed your ftudies, I doubt whether you can produce many inftances in which the political apoftate,

B   inftead

inftead of the language which becomes his wretched fituation, dares to affume the tone of parade and of triumph ; and with the moft eccentric originality of infolence labours to convert his own defertion of principle into an argument againft thefe principles themfelves, inftead of feeling the principles as a *ftigma* on his defertion. We do not find that Curio was fhamelefs enough, when he deferted the caufe of his country, to urge againft it the boldnefs of his own apoftacy with the fame confidence that Cato would have ufed in its fupport the authority of his virtue. The annals of ancient or modern apoftacy contain nothing fo flagrant. It was referved for our days to add this variety to the various combinations of fraud and infoience, which have in former ages duped and oppreffed mankind; and it was peculiarly referved for a Statefman, whofe character reconciles the moft repugnant extremes of political depravity, the pliancy of the moft abject intrigue, with the vaunting of the moft lofty hypocrify. It was referved served for him, not alone silently to abandon, not alone even publicly to abjure the doctrines of his former life; not alone to oppose, with ardour, with vehemence, with virulence, those propositions from others, by which he himself had earned unmerited popularity, and climbed to unexampled power; but by a refinement of insolent apostacy, to convert into a source of obloquy against other men, a measure which had been the basis of his own reputation and importance. It was reserved for such a man to repeat those very common-place objections to the measure, and those very common-place slanders against its movers which had been urged against himself, and which he himself had justly despised, or victoriously refuted *. It was reserved for him, unblushingly

* See the debate on Mr. Pitt's motion for Parliamentary Reform on the 7th May, 1782. Compare the reply of the Chancellor of the Exchequer to the alarms and arguments of Mr. T. Pitt, *proprietor of Old Sarum,* with his speech on the notice of Mr. Grey, the 30th April, 1792, in which he

expresses

blushingly to renew all the clamour against novelty, and all those affectionate alarms for the British Constitution, which patriotic borough-mongers had so successfully employed against himself. Yes, Sir, it was reserved for the son of Chatham thus to stigmatize the " dying legacy" of his father, and thus to brand his own " virgin effort."

You will have already perceived, that it is on your late conduct in the case of Parliamentary Reform, that I am about to animadvert. Though I feel a dislike not unmixed with contempt for politics purely personal, and though I should be the last man to betray and degrade the great cause of Reform, by mingling it with the petty squabbles of party, yet when I see the authority of an apostate character opposed with impudent absurdity to the cause from which he apostatized,

expresses those alarms which he had then scouted, and retails those arguments which he had then contemned !—*Ergo referens hæc nuncius ibit Pelidæ genitori !*

I think

I think it at least fit that that obstacle should be removed, and that the vapouring language of such a delinquent should be counteracted by the merited brand of his crimes.

The cause of Reform demands that the nature of your present opposition to it should be understood by the people. The interest of the people demands that they should well understand the character of him who may yet be likely, in some possible combination of events, to offer himself to them as the champion of Reform, and perhaps ultimately to prove the leader in more extensive and dangerous measures. And it is generally fit that no signal example of triumphant apostacy should pass with impunity.

These are the public reasons, Sir, which lead me to call public attention to your conduct; reasons which have influenced one who has no respect for your principles, and no exaggerated opinion of your abilities, which he has some-

times

times admired without idolatry, and often oppofed without fear. That I am in no abject or
devoted fenfe a partizan, I truft even my prefent
fentiments will prove. I am only, therefore,
your enemy fo far as I believe you to be the enemy of my country; and I am not unwilling to
adopt for the creed of my *perfonal* politics the
dying prayer of a great man, " *Ut ita cuique eve-
niat ut quifque de Republica mereatur ?*"

The three general grounds then on which I
fhall proceed to examine your conduct are, your
apoftacy—your prefent pretexts for oppofing reform—and the probability of fuch a future conduct in you as may render it extremely important that the people fhould juftly appreciate
your character.

Your entrance into public life was marked by
circumftances more favourable than any Englifh
Statefman has ever experienced. With all the
vigor

vigor of your own talents, with all the reflected
luftre of your Father's character, you appeared
at a moment when the ungracious toil of oppofition was almoft paft, when little remained but to
profit by the effect of other men's efforts, and
to urge the 'fall of a tottering Miniftry, whofe
mifconduct had already been fatally proved by
national misfortune. The current of popularity
had already fet ftrongly againft the Minifter.
The illufions of American conqueft and American revenue were difpelled. The eyes of the
people were opened to the folly of the Cabinet.
You had only to declaim againft it. The attention of the people was called to thofe defects in
their Conftitution, which permitted fuch a Cabinet fo long to betray the public intereft, and
to brave the public opinion. You had only to
put yourfelf at the head of the people, to declare
yourfelf the Leader of Reform. In this character you had recourfe to the fame means, and you
were affailed by the fame objections, with every
paft and every future Leader of Reform. De-

fpairing

fpairing that a corrupt body fhould fpontaneoufly reform itfelf, you invited the interpofition of the people. You knew that difperfed effort muft be unavailing. You therefore encouraged them to affociate. You were not deterred from appealing to the people by fuch miferable common places of reproach as thofe of advertifing for grievances, diffufing difcontents, and provoking fedition. You well knew that in the vocabulary of corrupt power enquiry is fedition, and tranquillity is fynonimous with blind and abject obedience. You were not deterred from joining with the affociations of the people by being told they were to overawe Parliament. You knew the value of a jargon that does not deferve to be dignified by fo high a name as Sophiftry. You felt for it that contempt which every man of fenfe *always* feels, and which every man of *fincerity* will always exprefs.

As you were regardlefs of the clamour againft the neceffary *means* for the accomplifhment of

your

your object—as you knew that whoever would
fubftantially ferve the people in fuch a caufe,
muft appeal to the people, and affociate with the
people; fo you muft have had a juft and a fupreme
contempt for the fophiftry which was oppofed to
the meafure of reforming the Reprefentation itfelf. You were told (every Reformer has been
told, and every Reformer will be told) that of
innovations there is no end, that to adopt one
is to invite a fucceffion; and that though you
knew the limits of your own Reforms, you
could not prefcribe bounds to the views which
their fuccefs might awaken in the minds of
others. To fo battered a generality it was eafy
to oppofe another common-place. It was eafy
to urge that as no Government could be fecure
if it were to be perpetually changed; fo no
abufe could be reformed if inftitutions are to be
inflexibly maintained. If they call the courage
of a Reformer temerity, he is equally entitled
to reprefent their caution as cowardice. If they
fpeak from conjecture of his future intereft in
confufion,

confufion, he may from knowledge fpeak of their actual intereft in corruption.

They told you that extravagant fpeculations were abroad*; that it was no moment to hope for the accomplifhment of a temperate Reform, when there were fo many men of mifchievous and vifionary principles, whom your attempts would embolden, and whom your Reforms would not content. You replied, that the redrefs of real grievances was the fureft remedy againft imaginary alarms; that the exiftence of acknow-ledged corruptions is the only circumftance that, renders incendiaries formidable; and that to correct thefe corruptions is to wreft from them their moft powerful weapon.

By a conduct thus natural you purfued your, meafure. Of that conduct indeed I fhould not now have reminded you, *had it not been for the*

* Lord Camelford's fpeech.

fake

*fake of contrafting it with fome recent tranfac-
tions.* It is almoft unneceflary to add that you
found it eafy to practife on the generous credulity of the Englifh people, and that for the firft
time in the prefent reign, the King's advifers
thought fit to chufe *their* minifter from the
knowledge of his being popular, actuated by
the double policy of debauching a popular leader, and of furrounding with the fplendour of
popularity, the apoftate agent of *their* will.
But with the other parts of your public life I
have nothing to do, nor will I trace minutely
the progrefs of your pretended efforts for Parliamentary Reform.

The curtain was dropped in 1785. The farce
then clofed. Other cares then began to occupy
your mind. To dupe the enthufiafts of Reform
ceafed to be of any further moment, and the
queftion itfelf flept, until it was revived by Mr.
Flood in 1790.

There

There was little danger of the fuccefs of his motion, maintained by himfelf with little pertinacity, and feconded neither by any Parliamentary connexion, nor by any decifive popular opinion. To it therefore you thought a languid oppofition from you fufficient. You referved more active oppofition for more formidable dangers, and you abandoned the motion of Mr. Flood to the declamation of Mr. Grenville, the logic of Mr. Windham, and the invective of Mr. Burke.

That more formidable danger at length arrived. A Reform in the Reprefentation was brought forward by a gentleman of the moft powerful abilities, of high confideration in the country, and of a character the moft happily untainted by any of thofe dubious tranfactions of which political parties are rarely able, for any long period to efcape at leaft the imputation. Such a character was odious to apoftacy. Such an enemy was formidable to corruption.

The

The debate on the notice of Mr. Grey illuf-
trated the fears of corrupt men, and the malignity
of apoftates.   It was then that alarms which had
flumbered fo long over incendiary writings were
fuddenly called forth by the dreadful fuggeftion
of a moderate, and therefore, of a practicable
Reform.

Nor is the reafon of this difficult to difcover.
Thefe incendiary publications might render fig-
nal fervice to a corrupt government, by making
the caufe of freedom odious, and perhaps by
provoking immatured and ill-concerted tumults,
the fuppreffion of which might increafe the
ftrength, and juftify the violence of Government.   No fuch happy effects were to be hoped
from the propofition of Mr. Grey.   Impracticable fchemes are never terrible, but that fatal
propofition threatened the overthrow of corruption itfelf.   Then your exertions were indeed
demanded : Then your pious zeal for the confti-
fution was called forth.

Theoretical

.

Theoretical admirers of the Conftitution had indeed fuppofed its excellence to confift in that trial by jury which you had narrowed by excife; and its falvation to depend on that liberty of the prefs which you had feared by profecution. Such might have been the idle ravings of Locke or Montefquieu. But you well knew its practical excellence to depend on very different things.

Already, in your imagination, that citadel of the Conftitution *Queenborough*, that fanctuary of freedom *Midhurft*, tottered to their foundations. Already, even *Cornwall* itfelf, the holy land of freedom, was pierced by the impious din of Reform. Actuated by alarms fo honeft and fo wife, for fuch facred bulwarks of the Conftitution, no wonder that you magnanimoufly facrificed your own character. No wonder that you ftooped to rake together every clumfy fophifm, and every malignant flander that the moft frontlefs corruption had ever circulated, or the moft ftupid credulity believed. Nor was it

even

even wonderful, when we confider it in this view, that you fhould have pronounced an elaborate, a folemn, a malignant invective, againft the principles which you yourfelf had profeffed, the precife meafures which you had promoted, and the very means which you had chofen for their accomplifhment. There is fomething in fuch a parade of apoftacy, which, in the minds of *certain perfons*, may efface thofe veftiges of diftruft and repugnance, that the recollection of a popular conduct in early life muft. have imprinted.

The difgraceful triumph of that night will indeed long be remembered by thofewho were indignant fpectators of it. A Minifter reprobating affociations, and condemning any mode of collecting the opinion of the people for the pur-pofe of influencing the Houfe of Commons.—He who commenced his career by being an Affociator, and who avowedly placed all his hopes of fuccefs in the authority which general

opinion

opinion was to have over the House of Commons. HE who continued a Minister in defiance of the House of Commons, because he
suppofed himself to poffefs the confidence of the
people. HE who gave the first example of legi-
timating and embodying the opinion of the
people against the voice of their reprefentatives*.
HE was the Minifter who adopted this language.
It was not, Sir, on that night to the fplendor of
your words, nor the mufic of your periods, that
you owed the plaudits of the borough-mongers
of Wiltshire or of Cornwall. They take no
cognizance of any dexterities of fophiftry or
felicities of declamation; the pompous nothing-
nefs of ABERCORN, and the fordid barbarity of
ROLLE, are more on a level with their under-

---

* These remarks are neither ftated to juftify or to condemn
the conduct of Mr. Pitt in the celebrated conteft of 1784.
They are merely intended to contraft his then meafures with
his prefent profeffions, and that any example of inconfiftency fo grofs and notorious is to be found in the black annals
of apoftacy, I am yet to learn.

standing

standing and more in unifon with their tafte. They applauded you for virtues like their own, for impudence in afferting falfehood, for audacity in defending corruption. Their affent was condemnation—their applaufe was ignominy— Their difgraceful *hear hims* ought to have called to your recollection the depth of infamy into which you had at length plunged. They were the very ufurpers whom you pledged yourfelf to your country to attack ; and at the only time of your life when your conduct had the femblance of virtue, thefe are the men in whofe enmity you would have juftly gloried. At that time your claim on the confidence of the people would have been almoft folely founded on the virulence of hoftility, and the vehemence of clamor which fuch men would employ againft you. And thefe *therefore* are the men whofe applaufe now juftly feals the fentence of your apoftacy.

Nor, SIR, is this brief hiftory of that apoftacy more flagrant than the plain ftatement of

your

your pretexts will appear, abfurd. The frank
and good-natured proftitution of DUNDAS,
which affumes no difguife, and affects no principle, almoft difarms cenfure, and relaxes us into
a fort of contemptuous indulgence for one whom
we can neither hate nor refpect. The unblufhing
fteadinefs of avowed Toryifm, whether it frowns
in Thurlow, or fneaks in Hawkefbury, we can
neither blame as inconfiflent, nor dread as con-
tagious. Many men may be intimidated by
their power, and many feduced by their corruption, but no man is deceived by their profeffions.
It is not therefore to fuch men that the FRIEND
of the PEOPLE defires to point their jealoufy and
their refentment. Againft fuch men it is not
neceffary to guard them. But it will, indeed,
be his duty to detect the *pretexts* by which the
fpecious and fuccefsful hypocrite not only dif-
guifes his own character, but triumphantly de-
ludes the people.

It

It is now then fit to examine thofe *pretexts* by which you would evade the ignominy of having deferted your caufe. Such a difcuffion is not only neceffary to convict you, but to the defence of thofe whom you have attacked. For unlefs the fallacy of thefe pretexts be expofed, the Friends of Reform may be branded as the thoughtlefs or malignant difturbers of their country, while the apoftate from Reform may be regarded as the provident and honeft preferver of its quiet. It is only by the expofure of his pretexts that this apoftate can be fhown in his genuine character, facrificing for the prefervation of corrupt power, not only the prefent liberty, but the future probable peace of his country.

Let us then, SIR, confider what thofe pretexts are, by which you labour to afcribe to infanity or profligacy in 1792, that attempt to reform, which in 1782 was the pureft exertion of the moft heroic patriotifm. By what fort of *chronological* morality virtue could fo fhortly

have

have been tranfmuted into vice, may be in itfelf
a curious enquiry. Has the generous enthufiafm of your youth been corrected by the jufter
views of experience? Has it been repreffed by
the felfifh coldnefs of advancing years? Or has
it been laid afleep by the genial indulgences, and
the feductive blandifhments of power? Such are
the queftions which a difcuffion of your pretexts
muft refolve.

You are in the firft place pleafed to inform us,
that thofe grievances which once fo clamoroufly
pleaded for a Reform of Parliament, have, under
your wife and virtuous Adminiftration, ceafed to
exift. The reafons, if we may believe the Duke
of Richmond and yourfelf, which then juftified
Reform, no longer operate. The nation is profperous. The people are contented. The ftatement of facts is as inconteftibly true, as the inference from it is impudently falfe. It is becaufe
the nation is profperous, it is becaufe the people
are tranquil, that this is an aufpicious moment

for

for averting from our country calamities which a corrupt House of Commons (by your confession) did *once* produce; and which therefore an unreformed House of Commons may again equally occasion.

The logic of apostacy is happily on a level with its morals. In 1782, when general discontent might indeed have furnished some colour for an alarm that Reform would degenerate into convulsion, then you and that noble Duke placed yourselves at the head of different bodies of Reformers. You suppose, it seems, that change is only to be attempted with safety, and bounded by moderation, when the temper of the people is inflamed, and exasperated by a succession of public calamities.

Such is the reasoning, such the politics of these honest Patriots, and accomplished Legislators! Other men might have supposed, that a state of convulsion and irritation was not the temper in

which

which moderate Reforms were likely to be adopted by the people; and that to defer all propofition of Reform until grievances fhould produce again fuch a fatal ftate, was to delay them to a moment when there would infallibly be no choice, but to take refuge in defpotifm, or to plunge into civil war. The very circumftance of the content of the people is that which gives us a perfect fecurity, that Reforms will not be hurried away into violence. It is therefore that which moft powerfully invites all men to exertion, who defire a wife and meafured improvement of the Conftitution.

Granting even that no *actual* or urgent evil arifes from the corrupt ftate of the pretended Reprefentation of the People—Granting that it has not within the laft eight years coft us thirteen Colonies, a hundred thoufand lives, and the accumulation of a hundred and fifty millions of debt—Making all thefe conceffions, what argument do they furnifh to you? Are the *neceffary*

tendencies

tendencies of an inftitution no reafon for reforming it? Is it becaufe thefe *tendencies* are fuf-
pended by fome accidental circumftance, that we
are to tolerate them until they are again called
forth into deftructive energy? Had you been a
Senator under,Titus, if any man had propofed
controls on the defpotic authority of the Empe-
ror, and if he had juftified his propofition by re-
minding the Senate of the ferocity of Nero, or
the brutality of Vitellius, you muft, on fuch a
principle, have oppofed to his arguments the
happinefs derived from the exifting Government,
till your fophiftry was confuted, and your fervility rewarded by Domitian,

It is thus eafy to expofe your pretexts, even
without difputing your affumptions. But it is
time to retract conceffions which truth does not
permit, and to prove that the abfurdity of your
conclufions is equalled by the falfehood of thofe
premifes on which they are eftablifhed.

C 4

The

The queſtion, whether thoſe grievances now exiſt, which in your opinion once juſtified a Parliamentary Reform, will be beſt decided by conſidering the nature of ſuch grievances, and the tendency of ſuch a Reform to redreſs them. The grievance is, the perpetual acquieſcence of the Houſe of Commons in the dictates of the Miniſters of the Crown. The ſource of this grievance is the enormous influence of the Crown in the Houſe of Commons. The remedy is, to render that Houſe, by changing the modes of its election, and ſhortening the duration of its truſt, dependent upon the people, inſtead of being dependent upon the Crown.

Such is the brief ſtate of the ſubject. Can you then have the inſolence to aſſert, that the influence has decreaſed in your time, or that it has produced a leſs abject acquieſcence? That influence and that acquieſcence are the grievances which are to be reformed; and as no impudence can deny that they exiſt in their full force, ſo no

ſophiſtry

fophiftry can efcape the inference, that the ne-
ceffity for reforming them remains undiminifhed.
Have majorities in your time been lefs devoted? Have the meafures of the Court been
lefs indifcriminately adopted ? Has the voice of
the people been lefs neglected ? Has the voice of
the Minifter been lefs obeyed ? Not one of thefe
things are true; not one, therefore, of the reafons for Reform have ceafed to operate.

But to argue the queftion in this manner is to do
injuftice to its ftrength. It is not only true that
the acquiefcence of Parliament has not been lefs
indifcriminate; it is not only true that the Houfe
of Commons have betrayed no fymptoms of fuch
ungovernable independence and impracticable-
virtue, as might feem to render its Reform lefs
neceffary or lefs urgent ; but it is uncontrover-
tibly true, that your recent experience furnifhes
a more fantaftic example of that ignominious fer-
vitude, from which Reform can only refcue the
Commons, than any other that is to be found in

our

our hiftory. I allude to your Ruffian armament, which I do not bring forward that I may fpeak of its abfurdity, becaufe I will not ftoop to wound a proftrate enemy, nor to infult a convicted criminal. I allude to it only as an example of the parade with which the dependence of the Houfe of Commons on the Minifter was exhibited to an indignant country. On former occafions it had been equally corrupt ; on former occafions it had been equally abfurd ; but on no former occafion had it difplayed fuch oftentatious and *verfatile* dependence. The Minifter in one feffion determines on his armament. His obfequious majority regifter the edict ; but the abfurdity, the odium, and the unpopularity of the meafure, fhake the refolution of the Cabinet. The voice of the people, defpifed by their pretended reprefentatives, is liftened to by the Minifter. The Houfe of Commons are at his nod ready to plunge their country into the moft ruinous and unjuft war ; but the body of the people. declare their fentiments, and the Minifter recedes. He

commands

commands his majority to retrace their fteps, to condemn their former proceedings, and thus to declare moft emphatically, that their intereft is not the intereft, that their voice is not the voice of the people. The obfequious majority obey without a murmur. " *Tibi fummum rerum judicium dii dedere—nobis obfequii gloria relicta eji.*"

Nothing could more forcibly illuftrate the mockery and nullity of what is ftrangely called the Reprefentation of the People, than this fplendid victory of public opinion. The Minifter yielded to that natural authority of public opinion, which is independent of forms of Government, and which would have produced the fame effect in moft of the fimple monarchies of civilized Europe. The Cabinet of Verfailles would have been compelled to exhibit a fimilar deference to the general fentiment before the fall of their defpotifm; and the people of England experienced no more aid from their fuppofed Reprefentatives, than if the Houfe of Commons had

been

been in form and avowal, what it is in truth and
fubftance, a chamber for regiftering minifterial
edicts.

Thus wretched are the pretexts to which you
have been driven. It is not only eafy to expofe
the emptinefs and futility of thefe pretexts, but
to eftablifh with all the evidence of which any
topic of civil prudence is fufceptible, that the
circumftances of the times, inftead of rendering it
dangerous to attempt a Reform in our Conftitution, make it infinitely dangerous to delay fuch
a Reform.

On the French Revolution, it is not my intention to offer any obfervations. It has no natural
nor direct relation to my fubject, and were I dif-
pofed to treat it, it would be my aim to attempt
what has not *hitherto* been attempted, and what
perhaps it may *yet* be too early to execute with
fuccefs, an impartial and philofophical eftimate
of the moft unexampled event in hiftory. But

on its *intrinfic* merits it is not now my province
to obferve. I have only to confider it as marking
the prefent time, either as aufpicious or inaufpi-
cious to attempts to reform our Conftitution.
Thefe attempts to obtain Reform difclaim all alliance with the magnificent principles, or the pe-
rilous fpeculations, by which men, according to
their various prepofleffions, will fuppofe our
neighbours to have been nobly animated or fatally
deluded.

Whether the boldnefs of thefe principles, and
the widenefs of thefe fpeculations, be as recon-
cileable with the order of freedom as they were
inftrumental in the deftruction of tyranny, is a
queftion on which wife men will not be prone to
anticipate the decifion of experience. But the
fchemes of Reform which we have now in view,
the only Reforms which, under the circumftances
I could approve, are founded on other principles,
on fentiments long naturalized among us, on notions of liberty purely Englifh.

Not

Not engaged either in the difcuffion or defence of the French Revolution, we then have only to contemplate it as it is fuppofed to render the prefent moment favourable or unfavourable to meditated Reforms in England. In this view it will be eafy to prove, that the probable future influence of that Revolution, *whatever be its if-fue*, on the general fentiments of Europe, marks the *prefent moment* as that in which a Reform of the Englifh Conftitution is not only fafe and prudent, but urgent and indifpenfible. Nothing indeed can be more evident, than that a mighty change in the direction of the public fentiments of Europe is likely to arife from that Revolution, whether it be fuccefsful or unfuccefsful. If it be fuccefsful, the fpirit of extreme Democracy is likely to fpread over all Europe, and to fwallow up in a volcanic eruption every remnant of Monarchy and of Nobility in the civilized world. The probabiiity of fuch effects is fo ftrongly believed by the enemies of that Revolution, that it is the ground of their alarm, the fubject of their

invective,

invective, and the pretext of their hoftilities. It
was to prevent fuch confequences, that Mr. Burke
fo benevolently counfelled the Princes of Europe
to undertake that *crufade* in which they are now
fo pioufly engaged.

If, on the other hand, the efforts of France be
unfuccefsful; if her liberties be deftroyed, there
can be little doubt that fuch a fhock will moft
powerfully impel the current of opinion to the
fide of Monarchy; a direction in which it will
be likely for feveral ages to continue. The example of the deftruction of the great French republic would diffufe difmay and fubmiffion
among a multitude, who only judge by events;
and the bloody fcenes which muft attend fuch a
deftruction, would indeed be fufficient to appall
the flerneft and moft ardent champions of Liberty. The fpirit of Europe would crouch under the dark fhade of Defpotifm, in dead repofe
and fearful obedience. The Royal confederacy
which had effected this fubverfion, would doubt-

lefs

lefs continue its concert and its efforts. The principle of maintaining the internal independence of nations, being deftroyed by the example of France, no barrier would any longer be oppofed to the arbitrary will of Kings. The internal laws of all the European States would be dictated by a Counfel of Defpots, and thus the influence of moral caufes on public opinion, co-operating with the combined ftrength and policy of Princes, " every faint veftige and loofe remnant" of free government will be fwept from the face of the earth.

In either alternative England cannot be exempt from the general fpirit. If the phrenzy of Democracy be excited by the fuccefs of France; if the fpirit of abject fubmiffion and of triumphant Defpotifm be produced by her failure, in the firft event the peace, in the fecond the liberty of England is endangered. In the firft event a furious Republicanifm, in the fecond a defperate Toryifm is likely to pervade the country. Againft

the

the prevalence of both extremes there only exists one remedy. It is to invigorate the democratic part of the Constitution; it is to render the House of Commons so honestly and substantially the representative of the people, that Republicans may no longer have topics of invective, nor Ministers the means of corruption. If the one spirit prevail, it is necessary to reform the House of Commons, that the discontents of the people may be prevented. If the other spirit prevails, the same Reform is necessary, that it may be strong enough to resist the encroachments of the Crown. In the one case, to prevent our Government from being changed into a pure Democracy; in the other, to prevent it from being changed into a simple Monarchy. In either event the same precaution is necessary. The same Reform will preserve the English Constitution from the sap of Royal influence, and from the storm of tumultuous Democracy. A Constitution which provided a pure representative of the people, and which included only enough of Monarchy for vigor, and only

D enough

enough of Ariftocracy for deliberation, would bid a juft defiance to the moft magnificent and feductive vifions of democratic enthufiafm. A people who felt that they poffeffed a vigorous popular control on their Government, could fee little obnoxious, and nothing formidable in the powers of the Peerage and the Crown, and would feel none of that difcontent which alone could make them acceffible to the arts of Republican miffionaries. The fuccefs of the French, the fafcinating example of their fuperb Democracy will have no dangerous effects on the minds of *contented* ENGLISHMEN. But what wifdom can avert the effects which muft arife from fuch a model of reprefentation, and fuch a fpirit as the fuccefs of France will produce in Europe, if that fpirit is to operate on a diffatisfied people, and that model be perpetually compared with the ruins of a free Government. In the alternative then of the fuccefs of the French Revolution, nothing furely can be fo indifpenfible as a fpeedy Reform in the Reprefentation of the People.

That

That to infufe a new portion of popular vigor into the Houfe of Commons is the only remedy that can be oppofed to the triumphant Toryifm which the fubverfion of the French Republic muft produce, is a propofition fo evident, as neither to demand proof nor to admit illuftration. We have feen the influence of an odious and un-popular Court victorious during a long reign, in hoftility to the prejudice, and in defiance of the jealoufy of the people. What then are we to expect from that increafed and increafing influ-ence, conducted perhaps with more dexterity in the Cabinet, feconded with equal devotion in the Houfe of Commons, and aided by the blind enthufiafm of a people, who are intoxicated by commercial profperity, and infatuated by all the prejudices of the moft frantic Toryifm? Under fuch a ftate of things, what can prevent the for-mation of an uncontroled Monarchy, and the abforption of every power by a Court, from which Englifhmen are to learn what remnant of perfonal fecurity it will vouchfafe to fpare, what

formality

formality of public freedom it will deign to endure, with what image of the Conftitution it will indulge and amufe an infatuated rabble.

Such are the effects which the fuccefs or the fubverfion of French Democracy feem calculated to produce on the temper and fentiments of the European nations. This therefore is the moment to repair and to ftrengthen the Englifh Conftitution. The fate of France hangs in fufpence. Her fuccefs is yet too dubious, widely or dangeroufly to diffufe a fpirit of imitation; and the conteft between her and the Defpotic League is ftill too equal to plunge the people of Europe into the lethargy of fervility or defpair. This then is that paufe of tranquillity, during which we have to prepare againft the hurricane with which we are menaced. This therefore is the moment when what was before expedient is become neceffary; when that Reform is now fafe, which in future may be impracticable or dangerous. Reform was before ufeful to improve;

prove; it is now neceffary (and perhaps the period of its efficacy is fhorter than we may imagine) to preferve the Government. Menaced by the predominance of a Democratical or a Monarchical fpirit, give the people their rights, and they will not be provoked to demand more; create an independent Houfe of Commons, and the power of the Crown will be checked; Defpotifm and tumult will be equally averted; the peace of the country will be preferved; the liberty of the country will be immortalized.

Such a moment muft have been chofen by a Statefman, who to an enlightened love for public tranquillity united an honeft zeal for political Reform. Such a moment therefore was not chofen by You. The opportunities which it furnifhed, and the public duties which it impofed, you neither felt nor regarded. But it afforded an opportunity of another kind, which you did not neglect, and of which, I muft confefs, you have availed yourfelf with no mean dexterity.

The

The difcuffions produced by the French Revolution had given birth to exaggerated ideas of
liberty on one hand, and had furnifhed a ground
to fome men, and a pretext to more, for exaggerated fears of anarchy on the other. No fuch fer-
ment of the human mind had ever arifen without
producing many extravagant opinions. Every
paffion and every frailty, in the ardor of difpute,
feduced men into extremes. Many honeft men
were driven into Toryifm by their fears. Many
fober men were betrayed into Republicanifm by
their enthufiafm. Such a divifion of fentiment
was precifely that which a good Minifter would
labor to heal; but which a crafty Minifter
would inflame into faction, that he might ufe it
to ftrengthen and extend his power. You had
to chufe under which of thefe characters you
were to pafs to pofterity, and you have made
your election. It was in your choice to mitigate
extremes, to conciliate differences, to extend the
mpartial beneficence of Government to all parties
and fects of citizens. But you chofe to take the
moft

moft effectual means to exaggerate extremes, to inflame differences, to give the fanction and countenance of power to one party, to put the Government of the country at the head of a triumphant faction. You diffeminated alarms of defigns to fubvert the Conftitution fo widely and fo fuccefsfully, that you have created in this country a fpirit of Toryifm more indifcriminate, more abject, and more rancorous than has exifted in England fince the acceffion of the Houfe of Hanover. Bigotry animates fervility, fervility mingles with the fear of confufion; the honeft fear of confufion becomes the dupe of the corrupt monopolifts of power ; and from the fermentation of thefe various paffions practifed on by your emiffaries, there has arifen a pufillanimous and mercilefs Toryifm, which is ready to fupport the moft corrupt Minifter, and to profcribe the moft temperate advocates of freedom. No fpirit could be fo valuable to a Minifter; nothing could enfure him fuch cheap and indifcriminate fupport. You could not fail

to

to recollect the happy ufe which the dread of Ja-
cobitifm was of to Sir Robert Walpole, and you
eafily faw that the dread of Republicanifm might
be. an equally fuccefsful engine in your hands.
The reformers of abufe are in fuch cafes called enemies to eftablifhment—The enemies of
the *Government* are to be called enemies of the
Conftitution. To have propofed the retrench-
ment of a *Tellerfhip* of the *Exchequer* from a
Walpole, was once to aim at the introduction
of the Pretender; to doubt the confiftency of
William Pitt, or to impeach the purity of
George Rofe! is now to meditate the eftablifhment of a democracy.

The progrefs of fuch a valuable fpirit you faw
with a joy which your hirelings boafted, which
your higher dependents but ill diffembled, and
which was even clumfily concealed by the plau-
fible and pompous hypocrify of your own character. What wonder that you fhould fee with
rapture and triumph the likelihood of even honeft

men

men gratuitously enrolling themselves among
your Janissaries—What did it import to you,
that in the mean while the phrenzy of Republi-
canism was likely to gain ground among a popu-
lace, provoked into wild extremes by the wild
extremes of their superiors? What signified the
dangers that might in time arise from the awak-
ening understanding of SCOTLAND, from the honest indignation of IRELAND? What were these
dangers to you! The Toryism of the higher
classes would *last your time*, and any collision
between the opposite orders in society, which
the diffusion of extreme opinions among them
might produce, was viewed without terror by
him whose heart had no virtuous interest in the
future fate of his country.

It had not however appeared necessary to declare by any overt act the alliance of Government with the favored faction, till an attempt
was made to mediate between parties, and to
avert the evils which impended over the country.

An

An affociation of gentlemen was formed for thefe purpofes. They erected the ftandard of the Britifh Conftitution. They were likely, by the liberality of their principles, to reclaim every thinking man who had been feduced into Republicanifm, and by the moderation of their views, to attract every honeft man who had for a moment been driven into Toryifm, They had already almoft effected an union of the friends of liberty and order, and reduced to a miferable handful the two extreme factions; the dread of one of which, and the fury of the other, were to be the inftruments of your power.

Such a danger demanded an extreme remedy. No man has more ftudied or more experienced the *gullibility* of mankind than yourfelf. You knew that the popular groffnefs would not diftinguifh between what it was your policy to confound. You therefore iffued a PROCLAMATION, which by directing a vague and indifcriminate odium againft all political change, confounded

in

in the fame ftorm of unpopularity the wildeft
projeEts of fubverfion, and the moft meafured
plans of Reform.

A Statefman, emboldened by fuccefs, and in-
ftruEted by experience in all the arts of popular
delufion, eafily perceived the affailable pofition of
every MEDIATORIAL party, the various enemies
they provoke, the oppofite imputations they in-
cur. In their labors to avert that fatal collifion
of the oppofite orders of fociety, which the diffu-
fion of extreme principles threatened, you faw
that they would be charged by the corrupt with
violence, and accufed by the violent of infince-
rity. It was eafy you knew to paint moderation
as the virtue of cowards, and compromife as the
policy of knaves, to the ftormy and intolerant
enthufiafm of faEtion ; and the malignant alarms
of the corrupt would, it is obvious, be forward
to brand every moderate fentiment and every mediatorial effort as fymptoms of collufion with the
violent, and of treachery to the caufe of public
order.

order. It scarcely required the incentive and the
sanction of a solemn public measure from the
Government to let loose so many corrupt interests
and malignant passions on the natural object of
their enmity. But such a sanction and incentive
might certainly add something to the activity of
these interests, and to the virulence of these paf-
sions. Such a sanction and incentive you therefore gave in your Proclamation. To brand me-
diation as treachery, and neutrality as disguised
hostility; to provoke the violent into new indif-
cretions, and to make those indiscretions the means
of aggravating the Toryism of the timid by awak-
ening their alarms; to bury under one black and in-
discriminate obloquy of licentiousness the memory
of every principle of freedom; to rally round the
banners of religious perfecution, and of political
corruption, every man in the kingdom who dreads
anarchy, and who deprecates confusion; to esta-
blish on the broadeft foundation oppression and
fervility for the present, and to heap up in store
all the causes of anarchy and civil commotion for

future

future times ; fuch is the malignant policy, fuch
are the mifchievous tendencies, fuch are the experienced effects of that PROCLAMATION. It is
fufficient that, *for the prefent*, it converts the
kingdom into a camp of janiffaries, enlifted by
their alarms to defend your power. It is indeed well adapted to produce other remoter
and collateral effects, which the *far-fighted* politics of the Addreffers have not difcerned. It
is certainly well calculated to blow into a flame
that fpark of Republicanifm which moderation
muft have extinguifhed, but which may, in future *conceivable circumftances*, produce effects, at
the fuggeftion of which good men will fhudder,
and on which wife men will rather meditate than
defcant. It is certain that in this view your Proclamation is as effectual in irritating fome men
into Republicanifm, as Mr. Paine's pamphlets
have been in frightening others into Toryifm.

Perhaps, however, the events which fuch a
fpirit might produce, are contingencies that enter
into

into the calculations of certain Statefmen. Perhaps they anticipate the moment when the Republican mob of the lower orders may be as valuable to them as the Tory vulgar of the higher
are now. Perhaps they may deem it a mafter
ftroke of Machiavelian policy to foment the ani-
mofity of two factions, one of whom maintains
the prefent Dictator, and the other of whom may
aggrandize the future Demagogue.

Such a policy is not altogether improbable ;
and if the eternal alliance of wifdom with virtue
could be broken, might not be thought altogether
unwife. The man who was capable of it would
not be deceived by the prefent appearance of
profperity and content. He would eafily fee, how
rapidly public calamity, acting upon Republican
theories, might change the fcene ; far lefs would
be hindered by the prefent appearances of furious
loyalty among fome of the lower claffes of fociety.
He would perceive this ftate of fentiment to be
the forced produce of artificial caufes, and he
could

could anticipate the violence with which they would rebound to an oppofite extreme, more natural to their fituation, more congenial to their feelings, and more gratifying to their pride.

The fuccefs of fuch a policy would certainly demand in the Statefman who adopted it an union of talents and difpofitions which are not often combined. Cold, ftern, crafty, and ambiguous, he muft be, without thofe entanglements of friendfhip and thofe reftraints of feeling, by which tender natures are held back from defperate enterprizes. No ingenuoufnefs muft betray a glimpfe of his defigns; no compunction muft fufpend the ftroke of his ambition. He muft never be feduced into any honeft profeffion of *precife* public principle, which might afterwards arife againft him as the record of his apoftacy; he muft be prepared for acting every inconfiftency, by perpetually veiling his political profeffions in the *nomeaning* of lofty generalities. The abfence of gracious and popular manners, which can find no

place

place in fuch a character will be well compen-
fated by the auftere and oftentatious virtues of
infenfibility. He muft poffefs the parade without
the reftraints of morals. He muft unite the moft
profound diffimulation with all the ardor of enterprize; he muft be prepared by one part of his
character for the violence of a multitude, and by
another for the duplicity of a Court. If fuch a
man arofe at any critical moment in the fortune
of a State; if he were unfettered by any great
political connexion; if his intereft were not
linked to the ftability of public order by any
ample property; if he could carry with him to
any enterprize no little authority and fplendor of
character; he indeed would be an object of more
rational dread than a thoufand Republican pam-
phleteers.

Againft fuch a man it would be fit to warn the
people whom he might delude, and the opulent
whom he might deftroy. Whether fuch be the
character of any living Statefman, it belongs to
History to determine.

I fhall dwell no longer on portraits that may be imaginary, and fpeculations which may be illufive. The dangers which have haunted my imagination may be unreal; but if ever fuch dangers fhould be realized in a moment of pub-lic calamity, and if public confidence fhould then be triumphantly feized by a convicted de-linquent, like the prefent Minifter of England; if the people fhould then forget the blackeft treachery to their caufe, and the meaneft ma-lignity againft their friends; then indeed the pa-rade of your confidence in popular folly will be juftified; and a contempt for the underftanding of the people will be proved to be the beft re-quifite for ruling them abfolutely, as well as the beft proof of having eftimated them correctly.

If fuch be the ftate of the People of England, no human power can fave them; they muft be abandoned to their misfortunes and to your delu-fions. In the confidence that they are more ge-nerous, and more wife, I have now arraigned

E   you

you before their tribunal. Events will decide whether my refpect or your contempt be beft founded, and the decifion involves the fate of liberty and of our country.

I will not conclude this letter with expreffions of refpect which I do not entertain, but I will clofe it with confidently afferting, that every line of it contains the unbiaffed fentiments of

AN HONEST MAN.

APPENDIX.

No. I.

OPINION OF MR. LOCKE ON REPRESENTATION.

" THINGS of this world are in so constant a flux, that
" nothing remains long in the same state. Thus
" people, riches, trade, power, change their stations, flourish-
" ing mighty cities come to ruin, and prove in time ne-
" glected desolate corners, whilst other unfrequented places
" grow into populous countries, filled with wealth and in-
" habitants. But things not always changing equally, and
" private interest often keeping up customs and privileges,
" when the reasons of them are ceased, it often comes to
" pass, that in governments, where part of the legislative
" consists of representatives chosen by the people, that in
" tract of time this representation becomes very unequal and
" disproportionate to the reasons it was at first established
" upon. To what gross absurdities the following of custom,
" when reason has left it, may lead, we may be satisfied,
" when we see the bare name of a town, of which there re-
" mains not so much as the ruins, where scarce so much
" housing as a sheep-cot, or more inhabitants than a shepherd
" is to be found, sends *as many Representatives* to the grand
" Assembly of Law makers, as a whole county, numerous

A   " in

" in people, and powerful in riches. This ftrangers ftand
" amazed at, and every one muft confefs needs a remedy.
" For it being the intereft, as well as the intention of the
" people to have a fair and *equal Reprefentative*; whoever
" brings it neareft to that, is an undoubted FRIEND TO,
" AND ESTABLISHER OF THE GOVERNMENT, and can-
" not mifs the confent and approbation of the community.
" 'Tis not a change from the prefent ftate, which perhaps
" corruption or decay has introduced, that makes an inroad
" upon the Government, but the tendency of it to injure or
" opprefs the people, and to fet up one part, or party, with
" a diftinction from, and an unequal fubjection of the reft."

Locke on Civil Government, Book II:
Chap. 13. *Sect.* 157, 158.

No. II.

OPINION OF MR. JUSTICE BLACKSTONE.

" THIS is the SPIRIT of our Conftitution : not that I
" affert it is in fact quite fo perfect as I have here en-
" deavoured to defcribe it ; for, if any alteration might be
" wifhed or fuggefted in the prefent frame of Parliaments,
" it fhould be in favour of a more COMPLEAT REPRESEN-
" TATION OF THE PEOPLE.

Blackftone's Commentaries, Vol. I. Page 171, 172.

Such is the confeffion extorted by the force of truth from
our cautious and courtly commentator.

No. III.

No. III.

Extracts from a letter written by the Duke of Richmond to Lieutenant Colonel Sharman, Chairman of the Committee of Correspondence at Belfaft, dated Auguft 15th, 1783.

" I have no hefitation in faying, that from every confide-
" deration which I have been able to give to this great quef-
" tion, that for many years has occupied my mind; and
" from every day's experience to the prefent hour I am
" more and more convinced, that the reftoring the right of
" voting univerfally to every man not incapacitated by na-
" ture for want of reafon, or by law for the commiffion of
" crimes, together with annual elections, is the only reform
" that can be effectual and permanent. I am further con-
" vinced, that it is the only reform that is practicable. The
" leffer reform (alluding to Mr. Pitt's motion in the Houfe of
" Commons) has been attempted with every poffible advan-
" tage in its favor; not only from the zealous fupport of
" the advocates for a more equal one, but from the affiftance
" of men of great weight both in and out of power. But
" with all thofe temperaments and helps it has failed; not
" one profelyte has been gained from corruption, nor has the
" leaft ray of hope been held out from any quarter, that the
" Houfe of Commons was inclined to adopt any other mode
" of reform. The weight of corruption has crufhed this
" more gentle, as it would have defeated any more effica-
" cious plan in the fame circumftances. From that quarter,
" therefore, I have nothing to hope. It is from the people
A 2

" at

" at large that I expect any good, and I am convinced that
" the only way to make them feel that they are really
" concerned in the bufinefs, is to contend for their full,
" clear, and indifputable rights of univerfal reprefentation.
" But in the more liberal and great plan of univerfal repre-
" fentation a clear and diftinct principle at once appears,
" that cannot lead us wrong. Not CONVENIENCY, but
" RIGHT. If it is not a maxim of our Conftitution, that a
" Britifh fubject is to be governed only by laws to which
" he has confented by himfelf or his reprefentative, we
" fhould inftantly abandon the error ; but if it is the effen-
" tial of Freedom, founded on the eternal principles of juf-
" tice and wifdom, and our unalienable birth-right, we
" fhould not hefitate in afferting it. Let us then but deter-
" mine to act upon this broad principle of giving to every
" man his own, and we fhall immediately get rid of all the
" perplexities to which the narrow notions of partiality and
" exclufion muft ever be fubject."

No. IV.

OPINION OF THE CITY OF LONDON.

Guildhall, Tuefday, April 11, 1782.

" AT a meeting of the Livery of London, appointed to
" correfpond with the Committees of the feveral counties,
" cities, &c. of the kingdom,"

Mr. ALDERMAN CROSBY in the Chair.

" Refolved Unanimoufly,

" THAT in the judgment of this Committee, unlefs a
" melioration of Parliament can be obtained, the beft official
" regulations

" regulations may foon be fet afide, the wifeft and moft vir-
" tuous minifters may foon be difplaced ; by the prevalence
" of that corrupt influence now fubfifting in the Houfe of
" Commons, which its defective frame naturally generates,
" and which has already fo nearly effected the ruin of this
" unhappy country."

No. V.

OPINION OF ASSOCIATED ENGLISH COUNTIES.

Extracts from the proceedings of a Meeting of Deputies appointed by the feveral petitioning or affociated bodies here-
inafter mentioned.

The counties of York, Surry, Hertford, Huntingdon,
Middlefex, Effex, Kent, Devon, and Nottingham, and the
city of Weftminfter, held on the 3rd day of March, and
by different adjournments on the 10th, 17th, 19th, 24th,
and 31ft days of March, and 21ft day of April, 1781,

" Refolved,

" That the parliamentary reprefentation of this kingdom
" is extremely inadequate."

" Refolved,

" That the extenfive public evils have been produced by
" the grofs inadequacy of the reprefentation of the people in
" parliaments."

No. VI.

Thatched Houfe Tavern, May 16, 1782.

" AT a numerous and refpectable meeting of members of
" parliament friendly to a Conftitutional Reformation, and
" of members of feveral committees of counties and cities,

PRESENT,

The Duke of RICHMOND,   The Hon. WILLIAM PITT,
Lord SURREY,   The Rev. Mr. WYVILL,
Lord MAHON,   Major CARTWRIGHT,
The LORD MAYOR,   Mr. JOHN HORNE TOOKE,
Sir WATKIN LEWES,   Alderman WILKES,
Mr. DUNCOMBE,   Doctor JEBB,
Sir C. WRAY,   Mr. CHURCHILL,
Mr. B. HOLLIS,   Mr. FROST,
Mr. WITHERS,   &c. &c. &c.

" Refolved unanimoufly,
" That the motion of the Hon. WILLIAM PITT, on the
" 7th inft. for the appointment of a Committee of the Houfe
" of Commons to enquire into the State of the Reprefenta-
" tion of the People of Great Britain, and to report the fame
" to the Houfe, and alfo what fteps it might be neceffary to
" take, having been defeated by a motion for the order of
" the day, it is become indifpenfibly neceffary that applica-
" tion fhould be made to Parliament by petitions from the
" collective body of the people, in their refpective diftricts,
" requefting a fubftantial Reformation of the Commons
" Houfe of Parliament.

" Refolved

" Refolved unanimoufly,

" That this meeting, confidering that a general applica-
" tion by the collective body of the people to the Houfe of
" Commons cannot be made before the clofe of the prefent
" feffion, is of opinion that THE SENSE OF THE PEOPLE
" SHOULD BE TAKEN AT SUCH TIMES AS MAY BE CON-
" VENIENT DURING THIS SUMMER, IN ORDER TO LAY
" THEIR SEVERAL PETITIONS BEFORE PARLIAMENT
" EARLY IN THE NEXT SESSION, WHEN THEIR PRO-
" POSALS FOR A PARLIAMENTARY REFORMATION
" (WITHOUT WHICH NEITHER THE LIBERTY OF THE
" NATION CAN BE PRESERVED, NOR THE PERMA-
" NENCE OF A WISE AND VIRTUOUS ADMINISTRA-
" TION CAN BE SECURE) MAY RECEIVE THAT AMPLE
" AND MATURE DISCUSSION, WHICH SO MOMENTOUS A
" QUESTION DEMANDS."

No. VII.

UNTIL the report of the Committee of the Friends of
the People on the prefent ftate of the Reprefentation fhall
appear, the following may ferve as a fpecimen of the
wretched tenure by which the privileges and liberties of the
People of England are now held.

" If we take the places where the majority of the electors
" comes below 20, it is fhameful what a proportion of the
" 513 (members for England and Wales) is fent into the
" Houfe by a handful, and that handful moftly people in
" low circumftances, and therefore obnoxious to bribery, or
" under the power of their fuperiors.

A 4

" Leftwithiel

	Sends members		Chosen by
" Leftwithiel —	—	2	—	13
" Truro —	—	2	—	14
" Bodmin —	—	2	—	19
" Saltash —	—	2	—	15
" Camelford —	—	2	—	10
" Bossiney —	—	2	—	11
" St. Michael —	—	2	—	14
" St. Mawes —	—	2	—	16
" Tiverton —	—	2	—	14
" Malden —	—	2	—	14
" Harwich —	—	2	—	17
" Thetford —	—	2	—	17
" Brackley —	—	2	—	17
" Banbury —	—	2	—	11
" Bath —	—	2	—	17
" Newport, Wight		2	—	13
" Newton, ditto —		2	—	1
" Andover —		2	—	13
" Gatton —		2	—	11
" Bramber —		2	—	8
" East Grinstead —		2	—	19
" Calne —		2	—	18
" Malmsbury —		2	—	7
" Old Sarum —		2	—	1
" Bewdley —		2	—	18
" New Romney —		2	—	17
" Marlborough —		2	—	2
" Buckingham —		2	—	7
		56		364

" Here

" Here we fee 56 members (about a ninth-part of the
" whole for England) are fent into the Houfe of Commons
" by 364 votes, which number ought not to fend in one
" member. For no member ought to be elected by fewer
" than the majority of 800, upon the moft moderate calcu-
" lation, in order to give 410,000 voters their due and
" equally diftributed fhare of legiflative power, without
" which equal diftribution the majority of the men of pro-
" perty are enflaved to the handful of beggars, who, by
" electing the majority of the Houfe of Commons, have fo
" great an overbalance of power over them, as to be able to
" carry every point in direct oppofition to their opinion and
" to their intereft."

Burgh's Political Difquifitions, vol. I. page 47—8.

No. VIII.

Sentiments delivered by Mr. Pitt on Parliamentary Reform,
in his fpeech in the Houfe of Commons, on Monday the
19th of April, 1785.

" HE faid he was fenfible of the difficulty which there
" was now, and ever muft be in propofing a plan of reform.
" The number of gentlemen who were hoftile to reform,
" were a phalanx which ought to give alarm to any indivi-
" dual upon rifing to fuggeft fuch a meafure. Thofe who,
" with a fort of fuperftitious awe, reverence the conftitution
" fo much as to be fearful of touching even its defects, had
" always reprobated every attempt to purify the reprefenta-
" tion. They acknowledged its inequality and corruption,
" but in their enthufiafm for the grand fabric, they would

" not

" not fuffer a reformer with unhallowed hands to repair the
" injuries which it fuffered from time. Others, who per-
" ceiving the deficiencies that had arifen from circum-
" ftances, were folicitous of their amendment, yet refifted
" the attempt, under the argument, that when once we had
" prefumed to touch the Conftitution in one point, the awe
" which had heretofore kept us back from the daring enter-
" prize of innovation, might abate, and there was no fore-
" feeing to what alarming lengths we might progreffively go
" under the mafk of Reformation. Others there were, but
" for thefe he confeffed he had not the fame refpect, who
" confidered the prefent ftate of reprefentation as pure and
" adequate to all its purpofes, and perfectly confiftent with
" the firft principles of reprefentation. The fabric of the
" Houfe of Commons was an ancient pile, on which they
" had been all taught to look with reverence and awe:
" from their cradles they had been accuftomed to view it as
" a pattern of perfection; their anceftors had enjoyed free-
" dom and profperity under it; and therefore an attempt to
" make any alterations in it, would be deemed by fome en-
" thufiaftic admirers of antiquity, as impious and facrilegi-
" ous. No one reverenced the venerable fabric more than he
" did; but all mankind knew, that the beft inftitutions, like
" human bodies, carried in themfelves the feeds of decay and
" corruption; and therefore he thought himfelf juftifiable in
" propofing remedies againft this corruption, which the
" frame of the conftitution muft neceffarily experience in
" the lapfe of years, if not prevented by wife and judicious
" regulations.

———————

" The argument of withftanding all reformation, from
" the fear of the ill confequences that might enfue, made
" gentlemen

" gentlemen come to a fort of compromife with themfelves.
" We are fenfible of certain defects; we feel certain incon-
" veniences in the prefent ftate of reprefentation ; but fear-
" ing that we may make it worfe by alteration, we will be
" content with it as it is." This was a fort of argument to
" which he could not give his countenance. If gentlemen
" had at all times been content with this fort of average, the
" nation would have loft much of that excellence of which
" our Conftitution now had to boaft.

" If there always had been a Houfe of Commons who
" were the faithful ftewards of the interefts of their coun-
" try, the diligent checks on the adminiftration of the
" finances, the conftitutional advifers of the executive
" branch of the Legiflature, the fteady and uninfluenced
" friends of the People, he afked, IF THE BURDENS
" WHICH THE CONSTITUENTS OF THAT HOUSE WERE
" NOW DOOMED TO ENDURE, WOULD HAVE BEEN IN-
" CURRED? Would the People of England have fuffered
" the calamities to which they had lately been made fub-
" ject?

" He needed not, he believed, to enumerate the argu-
" ments that prefented themfelves to his mind in favor of
" a reform. Every gentleman who had taken pains to in-
" veftigate the fubject, muft fee that it was moft materially
" wanted. To conquer the corruption that exifted in thofe
" decayed boroughs, he believed that gentlemen would ac-
" knowledge to be impoffible. The temptation were too
" great for poverty to refift, and the confequence of this cor-
" ruption was fo vifible, that fome plan of reforming the bo-
" roughs had clearly become abfolutely neceffary. In times
" of

" of calamity and diftrefs, how truly important was it to the
" people of this country that the Houfe of Commons
" fhould fympathize with themfelves, and that their inte-
" refts fhould be indiffoluble? It was moft material that
" the People fhould have confidence in their own branch of
" the Legiflature ; the force of the Conftitution, as well as
" its beauty, depended on that confidence, and on the union
" and fympathy which exifted between the conftituent and
" reprefentative. The fource of our glory and the mufcles
" of our ftrength were the pure character of freedom
" which our Conftitution bore. To leffen that character,
" to taint it, was to take from our vitals a part of their vi-
" gor, and to leffen not only our importance but our
" energy with our neighbours.

    " The purity of reprefentation was the only true and per-
" manent fource of fuch confidence ; for though occafion-
" ally bright characters had arifen, who, in fpite of the ge-
" neral corruption and depravity of the day in which they
" lived, had manifefted the fuperior influence of integrity
" and virtue, and had forced both Parliament and People to
" countenance their Adminiftration ; yet it would be un-
" wife for the People of England to leave their fate to the
" chance of fuch characters often arifing, when prudence
" muft dictate that the certain way of fecuring their pro-
" perties and freedom was to purify the fources of reprefen-
" tation, and to eftablifh that ftrict relation between them-
" felves and the Houfe of Commons which it was the ori-
" ginal idea of the Conftitution to create. He hoped that
" the plan which he had mentioned was likely to re-efta-
" blifh fuch a relation ; and he recommended to gentlemen
" not to fuffer their minds to be alarmed by unneceffary
                                  fears.

" fears. NOTHING WAS SO HURTFUL TO IMPROVEMENT
" AS THE FEAR OF BEING CARRIED FARTHER THAN
" THE PRINCIPLE ON WHICH A PERSON SET OUT.

" It was common for gentlemen to reafon with them-
" felves, and to fay that they would have no objection to go
" fo far, and no farther, if they were fure, that in counte-
" nancing the firft ftep, they might not either be led them-
" felves, or lead others farther than they intended to go.
" So much they were apt to fay was right—fo far they
" would go—of fuch a fcheme they approved—but fearing
" that it might be carried too far, they defifted from doing
" even what they conceived to be proper. He deprecated
" this conduct, and hoped that gentlemen would come to
" the confideration of this bufinefs, without fearing that it
" would lead to confequences that would either ruin or
" alarm us."

Debrett's Parliamentary Regifter for 1785, *p.* 43, *et feq.*

No. IX.

Extracts from the fpeech of Mr. Thomas Pitt, Propri- etor of Old Sarum, on the 7th of May 1783.	Extracts from the fpeech of the Right Hon. William Pitt, Chancellor of the Ex- chequer, on the 30th of April, 1792.
" THAT his honorable " friend had truly ftated that " the principal objection that " had been urged to what he " then propofed. the going in- " to	" It was obvious, Mr. Pitt " faid, to every rational and " reflecting man, that two " objects prefent themfelves " for

" to a committee to examine
" into the state of the repre-
" sentation, was that no spe-
" cific remedy was then sub-
" mitted to the House; and
" that at a time when wild
" and impracticable ideas of
" reform, and visionary spe-
" culations of imagined rights
" were floating on the pub-
" lic, such a committee
" would tend to alarm the
" minds of sober men, to in-
" flame the madness of theo-
" rists, and to hold out expec-
" tations that neither could,
" nor ought, nor were in-
" tended to be satisfied.

" That it was true that the
" temper of the times, was a
" very great additional ground
" to the opposition which he
" gave to the former motion:
" and that he certainly could
" have wished, that what-
" ever alterations were to
" take place could have been
" brought on at a time,
" when men's minds were
" less heated by speculative
" opinions; that however he
" could

" for their confideration; the
" first, the probability of car-
" rying a Reform in Parlia-
" ment at all; and the other,
" whether or not that Re-
" form, if carried, would not
" be attended with a risk
" that would outweigh the
" advantages that might ac-
" crue from it. To the first,
" he declared, he did not
" think that Gentlemen
" would readily be perfuaded
" to believe by what they
" had seen, and by what they
" knew, that there existed
" any alteration in the minds
" of the people tending to
" shew that a change in their
" Representation would be
" agreeable to their wishes;
" there was infinitely greater
" reason to believe that an
" attempt to carry any scheme
" into effect would produce
" consequences to which no
" man can look without hor-
" ror and apprehension.

" That there were out of
" that House men who were
" anxious to destroy the Con-
" stitution

" could not but congratulate
" that Houfe, and the coun-
" try in general, that thefe
" dangerous doctrines were
" difavowed by a perfon of
" the weight of the right ho-
" norable mover of thefe re-
" folutions, as well in what
" he had fo ably ftated in his
" opening, as in the propofi-
" tions themfelves; which if
" adopted by the Houfe,
" would ftand as the ftrongeft
" proteft againft thefe wild
" fpeculations. That an ho-
" norable friend of his (Mr.
" Powys) had read fuch ex-
" tracts from fome of thefe
" incendiaries, as could not
" fail to make known the
" tendency of their tenets;
" that he had never thought,
" with all the induftry that
" had been ufed, that fuch
" opinions had extended very
" far in the body of the peo-
" ple; and that he was con-
" vinced, that even by the
" interval of a few months
" they

" ftitution he was perfectly
" ready to admit: that their
" numbers were great, or
" their power vigorous he was
" happy enough to doubt;
" their force, he was perfuad-
" ed, if it fhould come to be
" oppofed to the found part
" of the Conftitution and its
" defenders, would be found
" to be weak and trivial. He
" did not, Mr. Pitt declared,
" deem the conduct of thofe
" Members of Parliament to
" be the moft meritorious,
" who agitated the propriety
" of a Reform in the fhape
" of an Advertifement in the
" newfpaper, * rather than
" by difcuffions in that
" Houfe; he would not,
" however, enter on that
" point, as he was willing to
" impute the beft motives to
" every man. As far, Mr.
" Pitt faid, as he had had op-
" portunities of learning the
" opinions of the people, and
" of obferving their condi-
" tion

---

* For the decency and confiftency with which the Right Hon. Gentleman makes this remark. See the Refolutions at the Thatched Houfe Tavern, No. VI. of this Appendix.

" they had already vifibly
" fubfided amongft many of
" the moft zealous.

" That he could not, at
" the fame time that he ap-
" proved of fuch an experi-
" ment, even in the prefent
" moment deny the weight
" of fuch arguments as were
" founded upon the unrea-
" fonable fpirit of innovation,
" which certainly his ho-
" norable friend could not
" fuppofe it was in his power
" to fatisfy by fuch concef-
" fions as thefe, or indeed
" by any practicable reform
" whatever. The clamor
" would not be appeafed by
" it among thofe who are the
" loudeft in their calls for al-
" terations ; he wifhed there-
" fore fincerely, that fome
" fuch plan had already taken
" place in times of more
" calm and fober judgment.

" tion, he had reafon to
" think them perfectly tran-
" quil and happy : the prin-
" ciples, however, that fome
" men had adopted, tended,
" he feared, to overturn that
" tranquillity, and deftroy
" that happinefs. In regard
" to that matter, however,
" he had a ftronger reafon
" for his conduct ; he was
" firmly convinced that the
" allies to whom the Hon.
" Gentleman was to look for
" fupport, were not thofe
" whofe object was to repair
" the Conftitution, but to fap
" the foundation, and deftroy
" the edifice ; they were per-
" fons who had condemned
" hereditary monarchy, a-
" bufed ariftocracy, and de-
" cried all proper and regu-
" lated Government what-
" ever ; men, who while
" they for one minute talked
" of a Parliamentary Re-
" form, libelled the Revolu-
" tion itfelf the other, who
" ridiculed the idea of rank
" and fubordination, and en-
" deavoured to imprefs upon
" the

" the mind of the public, a
" defire to fubftitute for the
" happy conftitution they at
" prefent enjoy, a plan found-
" ed on what was abfurdly
" termed the Rights of Man ;
" a plan which never exifted
" in any part of the habitable
" globe, and which, if it
" fhould exift in the morn-
" ing, muft perifh ere fun-
" fet; as muft be the inevita-
" ble fate of the government
" of any kingdom which
" fhould be formed on that
" abfurd and impracticable
" fyftem. To the laft hour
" of his life, Mr. Pitt de-
" clared, he was determined
" to maintain and defend
" the Conftitution of his
" country, for he was
" convinced that it was the
" beft that ever was formed
" for the happinefs of men :
" and he was convinced that
" there exifted no chance of
" fuccefs from the proceed-
" ings of the Hon. Gentle-
" man, and from any frauds
" which might be practifed,
" but that they tended to rifk

F   " the

" the incurring confequences
" the moft dreadful. Were
" he put to the difagreeable
" alternative of giving his
" vote for ever to forego re-
" form, or to rifk the inevit-
" able and dreadful confe-
" quences which would arife
" from the attempts, if per-
" mitted, of the new reform-
" ers, he declared upon his
" honour, as an Englifh-
" man, and as a friend to
" the Conftitution, that he
" fhould have no doubt of
" voting the former. Thus
" much, Mr. Pitt faid, he
" had offered as to the *time* of
" bringing forward the bufi-
" nefs, which, when coupled
" with the *mode*, rendered it
" ftill more dangerous. The
" minds of men were led
" to no plan, nor had they
" any grievance ftated to
" them. Their opinions
" were fet afloat, * and their
" underftandings were endea-
" voured to be poifoned by

* The Reader is again requefted to ftudy the character of Mr. Pitt in the contraft between this affertion and the Thatched Houfe Refolution.

" the

" the general aſſertion of the
" exiſtence of grievances,
" and the inadequacy of the
" Repreſentation in Parlia-
" ment: they had that held
" out to them as innocent
" and harmleſs, which was de-
" ſtructive and iniquitous."

FINIS.

www.ingramcontent.com/pod-product-compliance
Lightning Source LLC
Chambersburg PA
CBHW020232090426
42735CB00010B/1666